THE FOURTH

– AND BY FAR THE MOST RECENT –

637

BEST THINGS

ANYBODY EVER SAID

Books by Robert Byrne

THE FOURTH

– AND BY FAR THE MOST RECENT –

637

BEST THINGS

ANYBODY EVER SAID

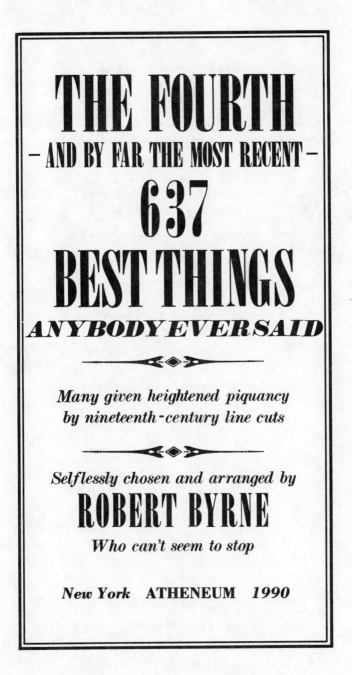

*Many given heightened piquancy
by nineteenth-century line cuts*

Selflessly chosen and arranged by

ROBERT BYRNE

Who can't seem to stop

New York   ATHENEUM   1990

Atheneum
Macmillan Publishing Company
866 Third Avenue, New York, N.Y. 10022
Collier Macmillan Canada, Inc.

Library of Congress Cataloging-in-Publication Data
The fourth—and by far the most recent—637 best things anybody ever said
p.   cm.
Includes bibliographical references.

1. Quotation, English.   I. Byrne, Robert, ———.
PN6083.F68   1990

082—dc20   89-29040
                                                                    CIP

PRINTED IN THE UNITED STATES OF AMERICA

*Dedicated with love
to anybody who has ever
invited me to dinner*

Contents

Introduction

PART ONE

God and the Universe, Life Itself,
Men and Women, Hair,
Love and Courtship, Blondes, Sex, Marriage,
Offspring, Christmas, Work, Success,
and that's just for starters

PART TWO

Lawyers and Money, Food and Drink,
Health, Politics, Celebrities and Boredom,
Sports, Books and Authors, Places,
Art and Music, War, Aging, Death,
just to mention a few things

PART THREE

One thing and another

Sources, References, and Notes

Index of Authors

Index of Subjects and Key Words

Introduction

What? Another collection of the 637 best things anybody ever said? Surely this time the bottom of the barrel
has been reached. Not so! Quality is still above the
bung, and much of it is in the cream zone. I think this
new assortment is as good as any of the previous three.
Readers who don't agree are invited to go back to what-
ever slime pit they came from.

Just kidding! I love my readers. Without them I
wouldn't be able to do what I do, the legitimacy of which
is borderline, in the opinion of my relatives. Hearing
from readers keeps me going—that and the money,
which has grown over the years to nearly a trickle. From
an R. G. Fisher in New Orleans: "Everyone knows that
life is not worth living, as Camus pointed out, so why
not waste it compiling meaningless quote books?" I
don't know. An attorney in Bucharest, Romania (the
farthest-flung fan to date), who has an indecipherable
signature, pointed out that "In every language there are
only 637 best things anybody ever said. The 638th is
always the start of another series of 637."

Another reader, on noting that I quote myself, suggested that "Robert Byrne should be gagged." Although
gagging wouldn't stop me from typing, the remark does
have merit and is therefore included in the pages that
follow.

Which is not to say readers are never a problem.
Take the case of the man who calls himself, for some

reason, Strange de Jim. He has contributed many splendid lines to Herb Caen's column in *The San Francisco Chronicle*, only two of which I repeat here. The problem comes with the Index of Authors. Is Strange his first or his last name? You'll find him alphabetized as Jim, Strange de.

Or take Hal Lee Luyah, who mailed me dozens of well-crafted zingers, five of which are included among the 637 presented here. Is Hal Lee Luyah a pseudonym or did his parents really call him that in order to have something to shout on Easter Sunday? He won't tell.

The reasons quality has held up are severalfold. One is that twice as much time—four years—was invested in compiling this sequel as in either of the previous two. Another is that the audience for them has grown, and a larger audience means more contributions. There are people who have sent me hundreds of their favorite lines. Such generosity is stunning. Beyond crediting and thanking contributors who have been especially helpful, I should send them some sort of prize or gift. Well, maybe not.

Third, comedy and comedians are growing in number and are churning out a river of material. Odds are that if you knock a random person down, it will be a standup comedian . . . or somebody who thinks he is. The country is awash in one-liners. Part of what I do is sit on the shore and take potluck from the flotsam.

A final factor is that I'm much older than I was when the series began and better able to pick quotes and drawings. There is more bile and acid in my blood. Socially and mentally, I'm much more twisted than before, doctors agree, and therefore in closer harmony with the rest of you.

A word about the antique line cuts, since nobody asked. They are taken from several dozen collections, most of them put out by Dover Publications, which contain between 15,000 and 20,000 drawings. It's not easy finding a good match between a quote and a drawing, and I think I deserve more credit than I've been getting. When I do find a match, I'm happy for up to a minute at a time, and my craggy face is wreathed in smiles. It's then that you should ask for favors.

A few announcements for readers unfamiliar with the earlier volumes: In Part One and Part Two, the quotes are loosely grouped according to subjects, which tend to follow one another according to the rules of life rather than the alphabet. For example, Hair follows Women, Loneliness follows Truth, and Boredom follows Celebrities. The result is a book best read from front to back, though browsing is permitted. Indexes are provided for those who want a quote on a particular subject or who are trying to locate a quote half-remembered.

Birth and death dates are given only for dead people. Quotes aren't numbered if they appeared in the earlier volumes or if they don't deserve a number. I don't know why certain topics are so much better represented than others, and I don't care. It's just the way it turned out.

I'm sorry about the number of quotes ascribed to Unknown. I relied more this time on contributions from readers, many of whom don't swing on scholarly apparatus. If you can supply a missing ascription, or correct a wrong one, or have a good line I missed, speak up. If you do send me something I can use in a future tome, you'll be mentioned somewhere in the text, a practice called *quid pro quote*.

For help in tracking down missing ascriptions, I wish

to thank Steve Allen, Stanley Ralph Ross, and Harry Crane. Thanks also to Abby Adams, compiler of the newly published *An Uncommon Scold,* who let me rummage through her manuscript in search of quotes by women.

Robert Byrne
c/o Atheneum Publishers
866 Third Avenue
New York, New York 10022

PART ONE

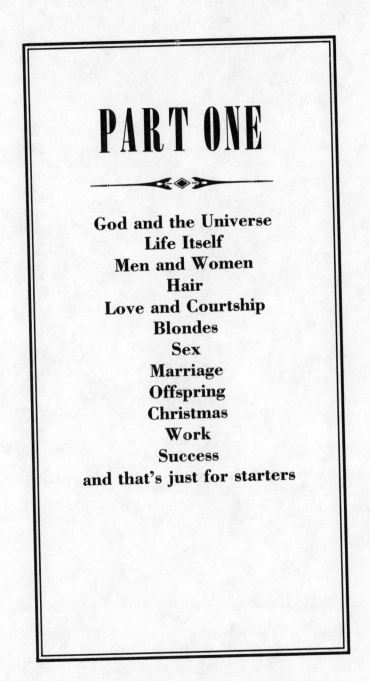

God and the Universe
Life Itself
Men and Women
Hair
Love and Courtship
Blondes
Sex
Marriage
Offspring
Christmas
Work
Success
and that's just for starters

1

God created man, but I could do better.

Erma Bombeck

2

If there is a supreme being, he's crazy.

Marlene Dietrich

3

Only two things are infinite, the universe and human stupidity, and I'm not sure about the former.

Albert Einstein (1879–1955)

4

We are here on earth to do good to others. What the others are here for, I don't know.

W. H. Auden (1907–1973)

5

I don't know, I don't care, and it doesn't make any difference.

Jack Kerouac (1922–1969)

6

There ain't no answer. There ain't going to be any answer. There never has been an answer. That's the answer.

Gertrude Stein (1874–1946)

7

The meek shall inherit the earth . . . if you don't mind.

Graffito

8

If you don't count some of Jehovah's injunctions, there is no humor in the Bible.

Mordecai Richler

9

Woe unto you who laugh now, for you shall mourn and weep.

Jesus Christ, according to Luke 6:25

10

I sometimes worry that God has Alzheimer's and has forgotten us.

Lily Tomlin and Jane Wagner

11

God seems to have left the receiver off the hook.

Arthur Koestler

12

If God listened to every shepherd's curse, our sheep would all be dead.

Russian proverb

13

What can you say about a society that says that God is dead and Elvis is alive?

Irv Kupcinet

14

To Jesus Christ! A splendid chap!

Toast by Sir Ralph Richardson (1902–1983)

15

If Jesus was Jewish, how come he has a Mexican name?

Unknown

16

Churches welcome all denominations, but most prefer fives and tens.

Unknown

1 7

The Vatican is against surrogate mothers. Good thing they didn't have that rule when Jesus was born.

Elayne Boosler

1 8

A difference of opinion is what makes horse racing and missionaries.

Will Rogers (1879–1935)

1 9

Do television evangelists do more than lay people?

Stanley Ralph Ross

2 0

Sin is geographical.

Bertrand Russell (1872–1970)

2 1

Even when I'm sick and depressed, I love life.

Artur Rubenstein (1887–1982)

22

Life! Can't live with it, can't live without it.

Cynthia Nelms

23

Life is something that happens when you can't get to sleep.

Fran Lebowitz

24

There is no cure for birth or death except to try to enjoy the interval.

George Santayana (1863–1952)

25

Why torture yourself when life will do it for you?

Laura Walker

26

It may be that we have all lived before and died, and this is hell.

A. L. Prusick

27

Life's a bitch, and then you meet one.

Unknown

28

Always look out for Number One and be careful not to step in Number Two.

Rodney Dangerfield

29

It's not what you are, it's what you don't become that hurts.

Oscar Levant (1906–1972)

30

The ethical argument regarding abortion hinges on the question of exactly when life begins. Some believe that life begins at forty.

Kevin Nealon

31

It is said that life begins when the fetus can exist apart from its mother. By this definition, many people in Hollywood are legally dead.

Jay Leno

32

Some mornings it just doesn't seem worth it to gnaw through the leather straps.

Emo Philips

33

Everything I did in my life that was worthwhile I caught hell for.

Earl Warren (1891–1974)

3 4

It's a dog-eat-dog world, and I'm wearing Milk Bone shorts.

Kelly Allen

3 5

You have to live life to love life, and you have to love life to live life. It's a vicious circle.

Unknown

3 6

In a fight between you and the world, bet on the world.

Franz Kafka (1883–1924)

3 7

Man was predestined to have free will.

Hal Lee Luyah

3 8

Swallow a toad in the morning if you want to encounter nothing more disgusting the rest of the day.

Nicolas Chamfort (1741–1794)

3 9

If you want a place in the sun, you must leave the shade of the family tree.

Osage saying

40

In spite of the cost of living, it's still popular.

Kathleen Norris (1880–1966)

41

If you're already in a hole, it's no use to continue digging.

Roy W. Walters

42

The longer you stay in one place, the greater your chances of disillusionment.

Art Spander

43

The optimist proclaims that we live in the best of all possible worlds, and the pessimist fears this is true.

James Branch Cabell (1879–1958)

44

An optimist is someone who thinks the future is uncertain.

Unknown

45

I always wanted to be somebody, but I should have been more specific.

Lily Tomlin and Jane Wagner

Dawn! A brand new day! This could be the start of something average.

Ziggy (Tom Wilson)

"That would be nice."

Charlie Brown on hearing that in life you win some and lose some.

Charles Schulz

The second half of the 20th Century is a complete flop.

Isaac Bashevis Singer

The more unpredictable the world becomes, the more we rely on predictions.

Steve Rivkin

There are few problems in life that wouldn't be eased by the proper application of high explosives.

Unknown

Reality is a collective hunch.

Lily Tomlin and Jane Wagner

52

Humankind cannot bear very much reality.

T. S. Eliot (1888–1965)

53

You've got to take the bitter with the sour.

Samuel Goldwyn (1882–1974)

54

Strife is better than loneliness.

Irish saying

55

Truth is more of a stranger than fiction.

Mark Twain (1835–1910)

56

It is annoying to be honest to no purpose.

Ovid (43 B.C.–A.D. 18)

57

Truth is the safest lie.

Unknown

58

I have seen the truth, and it doesn't make sense.

Unknown

59

Never let a computer know you're in a hurry.

Unknown

60

My theory of evolution is that Darwin was adopted.

Steven Wright

61

Never try to walk across a river just because it has an average depth of four feet.

Martin Friedman

62

Physics lesson: When a body is submerged in water, the phone rings.

Unknown

63

I like trees because they seem more resigned to the way they have to live than other things do.

Willa Cather (1873–1947)

I am at two with nature.

Woody Allen

Men are nicotine-soaked, beer-besmirched, whiskey-greased, red-eyed devils.

Carry Nation (1846–1911)

Many men die at twenty-five and aren't buried until they are seventy-five.

Benjamin Franklin (1706–1790)

Men are superior to women. For one thing, they can urinate from a speeding car.

Will Durst

Men are irrelevant.

Fay Weldon

I require three things in a man. He must be handsome, ruthless, and stupid.

Dorothy Parker (1893–1967)

His mother should have thrown him away and kept the stork.

Mae West (1892–1980)

I have yet to hear a man ask for advice on how to combine marriage and a career.

Gloria Steinem

When a man brings his wife flowers for no reason— there's a reason.

Molly McGee

Men! You can't live with them and you can't
1. Dip them in batter for tempura,
2. Use them for collateral on a loan,
3. Put in new batteries.

"Sylvia" (Nicole Hollander)

74

The main difference between men and women is that men are lunatics and women are idiots.

Rebecca West (1892–1983)

75

Any young man who is unmarried at the age of twenty-one is a menace to the community.

Brigham Young (1801–1877)

76

Talking with a man is like trying to saddle a cow. You work like hell, but what's the point?

Gladys Upham

Men read maps better than women because only men can understand the concept of an inch equaling a hundred miles.

Roseanne Barr

A dork is a dork is a dork.

Judy Markey

I have known more men destroyed by the desire to have wife and child and to keep them in comfort than I have seen destroyed by drink and harlots.

William Butler Yeats (1865–1939)

I grew up to have my father's looks, my father's speech patterns, my father's posture, my father's opinions, and my mother's contempt for my father.

Jules Feiffer

A woman who takes things from a man is called a girlfriend. A man who takes things from a woman is called a gigolo.

Ruthie Stein

82

The main result of feminism has been the Dutch Treat.

Nora Ephron

83

Men should think twice before making widowhood women's only path to power.

Gloria Steinem

84

You make the beds, you do the dishes, and six months later you have to start all over again.

Joan Rivers

85

Women have the feeling that since they didn't make the rules, the rules have nothing to do with them.

Diane Johnson

86

Women are cursed, and men are the proof.

Roseanne Barr

87

When a woman behaves like a man, why doesn't she behave like a nice man?

Edith Evans (1888–1976)

If a woman has to choose between catching a fly ball and saving an infant's life, she will choose to save the infant's life without even considering if there are men on base.

Dave Barry

Woman in Hurricane Has Same Baby Three Times
Tabloid headline suggested by Tracey Ullman

Women can do any job men can and give birth while doing it.

Allan Heavey

Women complain about premenstrual syndrome, but I think of it as the only time of the month I can be myself.

Roseanne Barr

My plastic surgeon told me my face looked like a bouquet of elbows.

Phyllis Diller

She was so ugly she could make a mule back away from an oat bin.

Will Rogers (1879–1935)

94

I don't consider myself bald. I'm simply taller than my
hair.

Tom Sharp

95

You're only as good as your last haircut.

Susan Lee

96

I am my hair.

Woman overheard by Roy Blount, Jr.

9 7

Every time I look at you I get a fierce desire to be lonesome.

Oscar Levant (1906–1972)

9 8

I hate people. People make me pro-nuclear.

Margaret Smith

9 9

Love is an exploding cigar we willingly smoke.

Lynda Barry

1 0 0

You need someone to love while you're looking for some-one to love.

Shelagh Delaney

1 0 1

God is love, but get it in writing.

Gypsy Rose Lee (1914–1970)

102

Abstinence makes the heart grow fonder.

Knox Burger

103

It is better to have flunked your Wasserman than never to have loved at all.

Jim Stark

104

Boy meets girl. So what?

Bertolt Brecht (1898–1956)

105

Men and women, women and men. It will never work.

Erica Jong

106

If you want to catch a trout, don't fish in a herring barrel.

Ann Landers on singles bars

107

The animals most often encountered in the singles jungle are pigs, dogs, wolves, skunks, slugs, and snakes. The fox is imaginary.

Robert Byrne

Robert Byrne should be gagged.

Tracy Chreene

108

I go from stool to stool in singles bars hoping to get lucky, but there's never any gum under any of them.

Emo Philips

109

A "Bay Area Bisexual" told me I didn't quite coincide with either of her desires.

Woody Allen

110

PERSONALS:
Famous Writer needs woman to organize his life and spend his money. Loves to turn off Sunday football and go to the Botanical Gardens with that special someone. Will obtain plastic surgery if necessary.

Sure-fire singles ad by Joe Bob Briggs

111

When I meet a man I ask myself, "Is this the man I want my children to spend their weekends with?"

Rita Rudner

112

Oh God, in the name of Thine only beloved Son, Jesus Christ, Our Lord, let him phone me now.

Dorothy Parker (1893–1967)

113

I enjoy dating married men because they don't want anything kinky, like breakfast.

Joni Rodgers

114

Women with pasts interest men because they hope history will repeat itself.

Mae West (1892–1980)

115

I turned down a date once because I was looking for someone a little closer to the top of the food chain.

Judy Tenuta

116

Have you ever dated someone because you were too lazy to commit suicide?

Judy Tenuta

117

Never date a woman you can hear ticking.

Mark Patinkin

There is one thing I would break up over, and that is if she caught me with another woman. I won't stand for that.

Steve Martin

My boyfriend and I broke up. He wanted to get married and I didn't want him to.

Rita Rudner

I'm dating a woman now who, evidently, is unaware of it.

Garry Shandling

Necessity is the mother of attraction.

Luke McKissack

When confronted with two evils, a man will always choose the prettier.

Unknown

123

Blondes have more fun because they're easier to find in the dark.

Unknown

124

When I was giving birth, the nurse asked, "Still think blondes have more fun?"

Joan Rivers

125

It is possible that blondes also prefer gentlemen.

Mamie Van Doren

126

Gentlemen prefer bonds.

Andrew Mellon (1855–1937)

127

Is sex better than drugs? That depends on the pusher.

Unknown

128

For birth control I rely on my personality.

Milt Abel

129

Condoms aren't completely safe. A friend of mine was wearing one and got hit by a bus.

Bob Rubin

130

When the clerk tried to sell me condoms that were made of sheep intestines because they have a more natural feel, I said, "Not for northern women."

Elayne Boosler

131

Some condoms are made of sheep intestines, but I was so scared the first time I wore the whole sheep.

Danny Williams

132

Some condom packages are stamped "Reservoir." You mean those things can generate hydroelectric power?

Elayne Boosler

133

National Condom Week is coming soon. Hey, there's a parade you won't want to miss.

Jay Leno

134

This gum tastes funny.

Sign on condom machine

135

"I don't know, I never looked."
Answer to the question: "Do you smoke after sex?"

Unknown

136

I don't even masturbate anymore, I'm so afraid I'll give myself something. I just want to be friends with myself.

Richard Lewis

137

The advantage of masturbation over intercourse is that it's less competitive.

Robert Byrne

138

Before sleeping together today, people should boil themselves.

Richard Lewis

139

Mr. Right is now a guy who hasn't been laid in fifteen years.

Elayne Boosler

I finally had an orgasm, and my doctor told me it was the wrong kind.

Woody Allen

141

My wife and I don't have mutual orgasms. We have State Farm.

Milton Berle

142

Erogenous zones are either everywhere or nowhere.

Joseph Heller

143

During sex I fantasize that I'm someone else.

Richard Lewis

144

I don't mind sleeping on an empty stomach provided it isn't my own.

Philip J. Simborg

145

"I don't know, what's the record?"
Answer to the question: "How horny can you get?"

Neil Simon

146

The difference between sex and love is that sex relieves tension and love causes it.

Woody Allen

147

I always thought of you as, at best, asexual, but maybe I was being kind.

From the television show "Slap Maxwell"

148

The late porn star Johnny Wadd claimed to have been
laid 14,000 times. He died of friction.

Larry Brown

149

I'm not kinky, but occasionally I like to put on a robe
and stand in front of a tennis ball machine.

Garry Shandling

150

Kinky sex involves the use of duck feathers. Perverted
sex involves the whole duck.

Lewis Grizzard

151

One figure can sometimes add up to a lot.

Mae West (1892–1980)

152

I wouldn't let him touch me with a ten-foot pole.

Mae West (1892–1980)

153

Mae West had a voice like a vibrating bed.

John Kobal

154

It's okay to laugh in the bedroom so long as you don't point.

Will Durst

155

Sex is a powerful aphrodisiac.

Keith Waterhouse

156

What do I know about sex? I'm a married man.

Tom Clancy

157

Some are born to greatness, some achieve greatness, and some have greatness thrust within them.

Hal Lee Luyah

158

Warning signs that your lover is bored:
1. Passionless kisses
2. Frequent sighing
3. Moved, left no forwarding address.

Matt Groening

159

I once made love for an hour and fifteen minutes, but it was the night the clocks are set ahead.

Garry Shandling

160

In the old days, women wore so many girdles, corsets, pantaloons, bloomers, stockings, garters, step-ins and God knows what all that you had to practically be a *prospector* to get to first base . . . to even *find* first base.

Danny McGoorty (1903–1970)

161

Ooooh. Ahhhh. Get out.

Andrew Dice Clay's impression of a one-night stand.

162

It is a gentleman's first duty to remember in the morning who it was he took to bed with him.

Dorothy Sayers (1893–1957)

163

I would never go to bed with a man who had so little regard for my husband.

From a novel by Dan Greenburg

164

Oysters are supposed to enhance your sexual perfor-mance, but they don't work for me. Maybe I put them on too soon.

Garry Shandling

165

My wife gives good headache.

Rodney Dangerfield

166

Oral sex is like being attacked by a giant snail.

Germaine Greer

167

Once while we were making love, a curious optical illusion occurred, and it almost looked as though she were moving.

Woody Allen

168

He gave her a look you could have poured on a waffle.

Ring Lardner (1885–1933)

169

In breeding cattle you need one bull for every twenty-five cows, unless the cows are known sluts.

Johnny Carson

170

After making love I said to my girl, "Was it good for you, too?" And she said, "I don't think this was good for anybody."

Garry Shandling

171

In sex as in banking there is a penalty for early withdrawal.

Cynthia Nelms

172

The mirror over my bed reads: Objects appear larger than they are.

Garry Shandling

173

I was a virgin till I was twenty, then again till I was twenty-three.

Carrie Snow

174

Losing my virginity was a career move.

Madonna

175

Sex after ninety is like trying to shoot pool with a rope. Even putting my cigar in its holder is a thrill.

George Burns

176

Sometimes a cigar is just a cigar.

Sigmund Freud (1856–1939)

177

This is my last year to fool around. Then I'm going to settle down and marry a rock star.

From the 1986 movie Modern Girls

178

Dating means doing a lot of fun things you will never do again if you get married. The fun stops with marriage because you're trying to save money for when you split up your property.

Dave Barry

179

There's nothing like a Catholic wedding to make you wish that life had a fast forward button.

Dan Chopin

180

I married the first man I ever kissed. When I tell my children that, they just about throw up.

Barbara Bush

181

Until I got married, I was my own worst enemy.

Unknown

182

The poor wish to be rich, the rich wish to be happy, the single wish to be married, and the married wish to be dead.

Ann Landers

183

Marriage is like paying an endless visit in your worst clothes.

J. B. Priestley (1894–1984)

184

Marriage is like a besieged fortress. Everyone outside wants to get in, and everyone inside wants to get out.

Quitard

185

The chains of marriage are so heavy it takes two to carry them, and sometimes three.

Alexandre Dumas (1802–1870)

186

Marriage is ridiculous.

Goldie Hawn

187

Instead of getting married again, I'm going to find a woman I don't like and give her a house.

Lewis Grizzard

188

Love is blind, and marriage is a real eye-opener.

Unknown

189

My divorce came as a complete surprise to me. That will happen when you haven't been home in eighteen years.

Lee Trevino

190

The secret of a happy marriage is to tell your spouse everything but the essentials.

Cynthia Nelms

191

All men make mistakes, but married men find out about them sooner.

Red Skelton

192

In marriage a man becomes slack and selfish and undergoes a fatty degeneration of the spirit.

Robert Louis Stevenson (1850–1894)

193

Conrad Hilton was very generous to me in the divorce settlement. He gave me 5,000 Gideon Bibles.

Zsa Zsa Gabor

194

The only thing that holds a marriage together is the husband being big enough to step back and see where the wife is wrong.

Archie Bunker

195

I've been married so long I'm on my third bottle of Tabasco sauce.

Susan Vass

196

There is nothing like living together for blinding people to each other.

Ivy Compton Burnett (1884–1969)

197

Always get married early in the morning. That way, if it doesn't work out, you haven't wasted a whole day.

Mickey Rooney

198

There are pigtails on the pillow in the morning that weren't there before.

Martin Luther (1483–1546) on marriage

199

I'm going to marry a Jewish woman because I like the idea of getting up on Sunday morning and going to the deli.

Michael J. Fox

200

That married couples can live together day after day is a miracle the Vatican has overlooked.

Bill Cosby

My wife and I were happy for twenty years. Then we met.

Rodney Dangerfield

202

My husband said he needed more space, so I locked him outside.

Roseanne Barr

203

You may marry the man of your dreams, but fifteen years later you're married to a reclining chair that burps.

Roseanne Barr

204

I grew up in a very large family in a very small house.
I never slept alone until after I was married.

Lewis Grizzard

205

My parents stayed together for forty years, but that was
out of spite.

Woody Allen

206

If it weren't for marriage, men and women would have
to fight with total strangers.

Unknown

207

Monogamous is what one partner in every relationship
wants to be.

Strange de Jim

208

Monogamous and monotonous are synonymous.

Thaddeus Golas

209

Monogamy leaves a lot to be desired.

Unknown

210

If you want monogamy, marry a swan.

From the movie Heartburn, *1987*

211

When Sears comes out with a riding vacuum cleaner, then I'll clean the house.

Roseanne Barr

212

My mom was fair. You never knew whether she was going to swing with her right or her left.

Herb Caen

213

As a housewife, I feel that if the kids are still alive when my husband gets home from work, then hey, I've done my job.

Roseanne Barr

214

My mother always phones me and asks, "Is everything all wrong?"

Richard Lewis

215

I'd get pregnant if I could be assured I'd have puppies.
Cynthia Nelms

216

Giving birth is like trying to push a piano through a transom.
Alice Roosevelt Longworth (1884–1980)

217

When I was born I was so surprised I didn't talk for a year and a half.
Gracie Allen (1906–1964)

218

I have never understood the fear of some parents about babies getting mixed up in the hospital. What difference does it make as long as you get a good one?
Heywood Broun (1888–1939)

219

A soiled baby with a neglected nose cannot be conscientiously regarded as a thing of beauty.
Mark Twain (1835–1910)

220

Babies don't need vacations, but I still see them at the beach.
Steven Wright

221

When childhood dies, its corpses are called adults.

Brian Aldiss

222

Adults are obsolete children.

Dr. Seuss

223

It's a dull child that knows less than its father.

Unknown

224

Before I was married I had three theories about raising children. Now I have three children and no theories.

John Wilmot, Earl of Rochester (1647–1680)

225

When my kids become wild and unruly, I use a nice, safe playpen. When they're finished, I climb out.

Erma Bombeck

226

My children love me. I'm like the mother they never had.

Roseanne Barr

227

The highlight of my childhood was making my brother laugh so hard that food came out of his nose.

Garrison Keillor

228

We had a quicksand box in our back yard. I was an only child, eventually.

Steven Wright

229

I was the kid next door's imaginary friend.

Emo Philips

230

As parents, my wife and I have one thing in common. We're both afraid of children.

Bill Cosby

231

My father was frightened of his father, I was frightened of my father, and I am damned well going to see to it that my children are frightened of me.

King George V (1865–1936)

232

If a child shows himself to be incorrigible, he should be decently and quietly beheaded at the age of twelve lest he grow to maturity, marry, and perpetuate his kind.

Don Marquis (1878–1937)

233

I reached puberty at age thirty. At age twelve I looked like a fetus.

Dave Barry

234

My niece was in *The Glass Menagerie* at school. They used Tupperware.

Cathy Ladman

235

Reasoning with a child is fine if you can reach the child's reason without destroying your own.

John Mason Brown (1900–1969)

236

There is nothing wrong with teenagers that reasoning with them won't aggravate.

Unknown

237

If Abraham's son had been a teenager, it wouldn't have been a sacrifice.

Scott Spendlove

238

If you want to recapture your youth, cut off his allowance.

Al Bernstein

239

Anybody who has survived his childhood has enough information about life to last him the rest of his days.

Flannery O'Connor (1925–1964)

240

Ask your child what he wants for dinner only if he's buying.

Fran Lebowitz

241

If you must hold yourself up to your children, hold yourself up as an object lesson and not as an example.

George Bernard Shaw (1856–1950)

242

My parents were too poor to have children, so the neighbors had me.

Buddy Hackett

243

Have children while your parents are still young enough to take care of them.

Rita Rudner

244

Children despise their parents until the age of forty, when they suddenly become just like them, thus preserving the system.

Quentin Crewe

245

Roses are reddish
Violets are bluish
If it weren't for Christmas
We'd all be Jewish.

Benny Hill

246

I stopped believing in Santa Claus when my mother took me to see him in a department store, and he asked for my autograph.

Shirley Temple

247

The three stages of a man's life:
  1. He believes in Santa Claus;
  2. He doesn't believe in Santa Claus;
  3. He is Santa Claus.

Unknown

248

You can't beat the gentiles in December. We were stupid to make Hanukkah then.

Ralph Schoenstein's grandfather

249

Santa Claus has the right idea: Visit people once a year.

Victor Borge

250

Thanksgiving comes *after* Christmas for people over thirty.

Peter Kreeft

251

Christmas is Christ's revenge for the crucifixion.

Unknown

252

Setting a good example for children takes all the fun out of middle age.

William Feather

253

There is no such thing as fun for the whole family.

Jerry Seinfeld

254

In order to influence a child, one must be careful not to be that child's parent or grandparent.

Don Marquis (1878–1937)

255

The time not to become a father is eighteen years before a war.

E. B. White (1899–1985)

256

A married man with a family will do anything for money.

Charles Maurice de Talleyrand-Perigord
(1754–1838)

257

To be a successful father, there's one absolute rule: When you have a kid, don't look at it for the first two years.

Ernest Hemingway (1899–1961)

Hemingway was a jerk.

Harold Robbins

Harold Robbins doesn't sound like an author, he sounds like a company brochure.

The New Yorker

258

You should have seen what a fine-looking man he was before he had all those children.

Arapesh tribesman

259

Parenthood remains the greatest single preserve of the amateur.

Alvin Toffler

260

I have over 42,000 children, and not one comes to visit.

Mel Brooks as The 2000-Year-Old Man

2 6 1

It behooves a father to be blameless if he expects his son to be.

Homer (circa 1000 B.C.)

2 6 2

Any father whose son raises his hand against him is guilty of having produced a son who raised his hand against him.

Charles Péguy (1873–1914)

2 6 3

Parents are not interested in justice, they are interested in quiet.

Bill Cosby

2 6 4

My parents only had one argument in forty-five years. It lasted forty-three years.

Cathy Ladman

2 6 5

My parents have been visiting me for a few days. I just dropped them off at the airport. They leave tomorrow.

Margaret Smith

266

I've been promoted to middle management. I never thought I'd sink so low.

Tim Gould

267

Do it my way or watch your butt.

Management philosophy from the movie
Raising Arizona, *1987*

268

No man ever listened himself out of a job.

Calvin Coolidge (1872–1933)

269

Canadians shouldn't come down to Southern California and take jobs away from our Mexicans.

Stanley Ralph Ross

270

There ain't no rules around here! We're trying to accomplish something!

Thomas Edison (1847–1931)

271

A career is a job that has gone on too long.

Cartoon caption by Jeff MacNelly

272

I used to work at The International House of Pancakes. It was a dream, and I made it happen.

Paula Poundstone

273

Tell your boss what you think of him, and the truth shall set you free.

Unknown

274

A holding company is a thing where you hand an ac-
complice the goods while the policeman searches you.
Will Rogers (1879–1935)

275

A criminal is a person with predatory instincts without
sufficient capital to form a corporation.

Howard Scott

276

The economy of Houston is so bad right now that two
prostitutes the police arrested turned out to be virgins.
Bill Abeel

277

Success isn't permanent, and failure isn't fatal.

Mike Ditka

278

Success has many fathers, failure is a mother.

Jeanne Phillips

279

The worst part of success is trying to find someone who is happy for you.

Bette Midler

280

Success is women you don't even know walking around your house.

From "Saturday Night Live"

281

If at first you don't succeed, find out if the loser gets anything.

Bill Lyon

282

Success in life means not becoming like your parents.

Louise Bowie

283

To make a small fortune, invest a large fortune.

Bruce Cohn

284

Formula for success: Rise early, work hard, strike oil.

J. Paul Getty, allegedly

The penalty of success is to be bored by the people who used to snub you.

Nancy, Lady Astor (1879–1964)

PART TWO

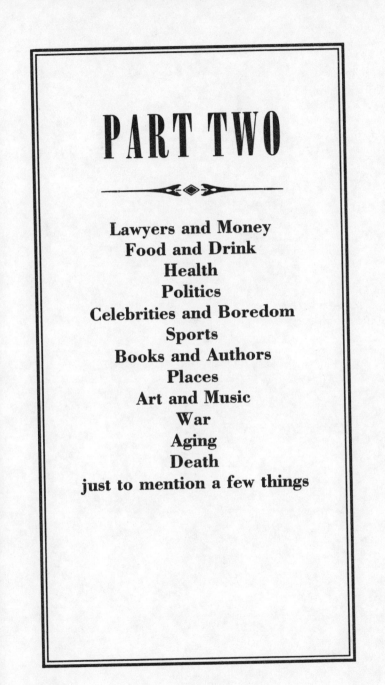

Lawyers and Money
Food and Drink
Health
Politics
Celebrities and Boredom
Sports
Books and Authors
Places
Art and Music
War
Aging
Death
just to mention a few things

286

Talk is cheap until you hire a lawyer.

Unknown

287

I've never been in love. I've always been a lawyer.

Unknown

288

There are three reasons why lawyers are replacing rats as laboratory research animals. One is that they're plentiful, another is that lab assistants don't get attached to them, and the third is that there are some things rats just won't do.

Unknown

289

A tragedy is a busload of lawyers going over a cliff with an empty seat.

Unknown

290

Lawyer Drowning in Bay Rescued

Headline nominated by George de Shazer as the saddest of the year

Lawsuit, n. A machine you go into as a pig and come out of as a sausage.

Ambrose Bierce (1842–1914)

292

Is it a bigger crime to rob a bank or to open one?

Ted Allan

293

Two can live as cheaply as one. Take the bird and the horse, for example.

Unknown

294

I don't like money, but it quiets my nerves.

Joe Louis (1914–1981)

295

I wish Karl would accumulate some capital instead of just writing about it.

Karl Marx's mother, allegedly

296

Money can't buy friends, but it can get you a better class of enemy.

Spike Milligan

297

Money won is twice as sweet as money earned.

From the movie The Color of Money, *1986*

298

Alimony is always having to say you're sorry.

Philip J. Simborg

299

Never get deeply in debt to someone who cried at the end of *Scarface*.

Robert S. Wieder

300

The rule is not to talk about money with people who have much more or much less than you.

Katherine Whitehorn

301

The way to make money is to buy when blood is running in the streets.

John D. Rockefeller (1839–1937)

302

I don't know much about being a millionaire, but I'll bet I'd be darling at it.

Dorothy Parker (1893–1967)

303

I don't have a bank account, because I don't know my mother's maiden name.

Paula Poundstone

304

I had plastic surgery last week. I cut up my credit cards.

Henny Youngman

305
Consequences, shmonsequences, as long as I'm rich.
Daffy Duck

306

A foundation is a large body of money surrounded by people who want some.

Dwight Macdonald (1906–1983)

307

The upper crust is a bunch of crumbs held together by dough.

Joseph A. Thomas (1906–1977)

308

I no longer prepare food or drink with more than one ingredient.

Cyra McFadden

309

Eternity is two people and a roast turkey.

James Dent

310

Do you hunt your own truffles or do you hire a pig?
*Conversational icebreaker suggested
by Jean McClatchy*

311

I refuse to spend my life worrying about what I eat. There is no pleasure worth forgoing just for an extra three years in the geriatric ward.

John Mortimer

312

I asked the clothing store clerk if she had anything to make me look thinner, and she said, "How about a week in Bangladesh?"

Roseanne Barr

313

Diets are mainly food for thought.

N. Wylie Jones

314

Avoid fruits and nuts. You are what you eat.

Garfield (Jim Davis)

315

I'm on a grapefruit diet. I eat everything but grapefruit.

Chi Chi Rodriguez

316

In two decades I've lost a total of 789 pounds. I should be hanging from a charm bracelet.

Erma Bombeck

3 1 7

The toughest part of being on a diet is shutting up about it.

Gerald Nachman

3 1 8

My idea of heaven is a great big baked potato and someone to share it with.

Oprah Winfrey

3 1 9

If it tastes good, it's trying to kill you.

Roy Qualley

3 2 0

Everything I want is either illegal, immoral, or fattening.

Alexander Woollcott (1887–1943)

321

Eating an anchovy is like eating an eyebrow.

Unknown

322

A favorite dish in Kansas is creamed corn on a stick.

Jeff Harms

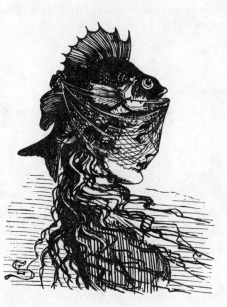

323

Meat is murder, but fish is justifiable homicide.

Jeremy Hardy

324

I smell a rat. Did you bake it or fry it?

Bill Hoest

325

Why should we take up farming when there are so many mongongo nuts in the world?

African Bushman quoted by Jared Diamond

326

You'll be hungry again in an hour.

Fortune cookie opened by Ziggy (Tom Wilson)

327

Your request for no MSG was ignored.

Fortune cookie opened by Merla Zellerbach

328

A vegetarian is a person who won't eat meat unless someone else pays for it.

Al Clethan

329

Cannibals aren't vegetarians, they're humanitarians.

Unknown

330

I'm not a vegetarian because I love animals; I'm a vegetarian because I hate plants.

A. Whitney Brown

3 3 1

Never order anything in a vegetarian restaurant that ordinarily would have meat in it.

Tom Parker

3 3 2

Where there's smoke, there's toast.

Unknown

3 3 3

Never eat anything whose listed ingredients cover more than one-third of the package.

Joseph Leonard

3 3 4

I don't eat snails. I prefer fast food.

Strange de Jim

It's okay to be fat. So you're fat. Just be fat and shut up about it.

Roseanne Barr

336

Come in, or we'll both starve

Sign in restaurant window

337

I hate to eat and eat and eat and run.

Neila Ross

338

Some people like to eat octopus. Liberals, mostly.

Russell Baker

3 3 9

Do not make a stingy sandwich
Pile the cold-cuts high
Customers should see salami
Coming through the rye.

Allan Sherman (1924–1973)

3 4 0

Plant carrots in January, and you'll never have to eat carrots.

Unknown

3 4 1

Ask not what you can do for your country, ask what's for lunch.

Orson Welles on reaching 300 pounds

3 4 2

Continental breakfasts are very sparse. My advice is to go right to lunch without pausing.

Miss Piggy

3 4 3

Miss Piggy is a boar.

Ed Lucaire

344

The key to a successful restaurant is dressing girls in degrading clothes.

Michael O'Donoghue

345

The food in Yugoslavia is either very good or very bad. One day they served us fried chains.

Mel Brooks

346

Good health makes the practice of virtue more difficult.

John Bunyan (1628–1688)

3 4 7

If you don't take care of your body, where will you live?

Unknown

3 4 8

Your medical tests are in. You're short, fat, and bald.

Ziggy (Tom Wilson)

3 4 9

How can I get sick? I've already had everything.

George Burns

3 5 0

When I told my doctor I couldn't afford an operation, he offered to touch up my X rays.

Henny Youngman

3 5 1

I quit therapy because my analyst was trying to help me behind my back.

Richard Lewis

3 5 2

The art of medicine, like that of war, is murderous and conjectural.

Voltaire (1694–1778)

353

Winston Churchill's habit of guzzling a quart or two a day of good cognac is what saved civilization from the Luftwaffe, Hegelian logic, Wagnerian love-deaths, and potato pancakes.

Charles McCabe (1915–1983)

354

I feel sorry for people who don't drink, because when they get up in the morning, they're not going to feel any better all day.

Frank Sinatra

355

I drink too much. Last time I gave a urine sample there was an olive in it.

Rodney Dangerfield

356

I never took hallucinogenic drugs because I never wanted my consciousness expanded one unnecessary iota.

Fran Lebowitz

357

Politics is a means of preventing people from taking part in what properly concerns them.

Paul Valéry (1871–1945)

358

Politics consists of choosing between the disastrous and the unpalatable.

John Kenneth Galbraith

359

Democracy is the name we give to the people when we need them.

Robert Pellevé, Marquis de Flers (1872–1927)

360

There has never been a good government.

Emma Goldman (1869–1940)

361

No more good must be attempted than the public can bear.

Thomas Jefferson (1743–1826)

362

Thomas Jefferson's slaves loved him so much they called him by a special name: Dad.

Mark Russell

363

When they asked George Washington for his ID, he just took out a quarter.

Steven Wright

364

George Bush is Gerald Ford without the pizzazz.

Pat Paulsen

365

A promising young man should go into politics so that he can go on promising for the rest of his life.

Robert Byrne

366

A politician is a man who approaches every problem with an open mouth.

Adlai Stevenson

367

A politician can appear to have his nose to the grindstone while straddling a fence and keeping both ears to the ground.

Unknown

368

My grandmother's brain was dead, but her heart was still beating. It was the first time we ever had a Democrat in the family.

Emo Philips

369

No matter what your religion, you should try to become a government program, for then you will have everlasting life.

U.S. Representative Lynn Martin

370

Most isms are wasms.

Philosophy professor Gerald Vision

371

We've upped our standards. Up yours.

Campaign slogan by Pat Paulsen

372

If I had known that my son was going to be president of Bolivia [in the 1940s], I would have taught him to read and write.

Enrique Penaranda's mother

373

Being head of state is an extremely thankless job.

Bokassa I, former emperor of the
Central African Republic, while on trial for
infanticide, cannibalism, and torture

374

If Roosevelt were alive today, he'd turn over in his grave.

Samuel Goldwyn (1882–1974)

375

When they circumcised Herbert Samuel, they threw away the wrong part.

David Lloyd George (1863–1945)
on a rival

376

Early today the senator called a spade a spade. He later issued a retraction.

Joe Mirachi

377

Voters want a fraud they can believe in.

Will Durst

378

A penny saved is a Congressional oversight.

Hal Lee Luyah

379

Are the people who run for president really the best in a country of 240 million? If so, something has happened to the gene pool.

Bob McKenzie

380

Nonviolence is a flop. The only bigger flop is violence.

Joan Baez

381

Nonviolence is fine as long as it works.

Malcolm X (1925–1965)

382

You're not famous until my mother has heard of you.

Jay Leno

383

The nice thing about being a celebrity is that, if you bore people, they think it's their fault.

Henry Kissinger

384

A celebrity is a person known to many people he is glad he doesn't know.

H. L. Mencken (1880–1956)

385

They want me on all the television shows now because I did so well on "Celebrity Assholes."

Steve Martin

386

People hate me because I am a multifaceted, talented, wealthy, internationally famous genius.

Jerry Lewis

387

In her last days, Gertrude Stein resembled a spoiled pear.

Gore Vidal

388

I don't like Diane Keaton anymore. She's had way too much therapy.

Patricia Wentz-Daly

389

It's sweeping the country like wildflowers.

Samuel Goldwyn (1882–1974)

390

Nominations in Most Boring Headline contest, sponsored by *The New Republic, 1986:*

Worthwhile Canadian Initiative (*New York Times*)

University of Rochester Decides to Keep Name (*New York Times*)

Surprises Unlikely in Indiana (*Chicago Tribune*)

Economist Dies (*Wisconsin State Journal*)

391

Every hero becomes a bore at last.

Ralph Waldo Emerson (1803–1882)

392

When I played pro football, I never set out to hurt anybody deliberately . . . unless it was, you know, important, like a league game or something.

Dick Butkus

393

Baseball is what we were, football is what we have become.

Mary McGrory

394

Go Braves! And take the Falcons with you.

Bumper sticker in Atlanta

395

Cal quarterback Joe Kapp used to call audibles that were just obscenities directed at the other team. I like that.

Stanford quarterback Greg Ennis

396

Yell for a losing football team:
Let's all jump and scream
For the lavender and cream.

Tom Batiuk

397

Baseball would be a better game if more third basemen got hit in the mouth by line drives.

Dan Jenkins

398

George Steinbrenner is the salt of the earth, and the Yankee players are open wounds.

Scott Osler

399

That's getting a little too close to home.

Bob Feller on hearing that a foul ball hit his mother

400

I'm not going to buy my kids an encyclopedia. Let them walk to school like I did.

Another thing never said by Yogi Berra

401

Pro basketball has turned into Wrestlemania, which is why I like college basketball and high school basketball. Actually, it's why I like baseball.

Frank Layden

402

No comment.

Doug Moe on hearing that he had been voted the most quotable coach in the National Basketball Association

403

If you are caught on a golf course during a storm and are afraid of lightning, hold up a 1-iron. Not even God can hit a 1-iron.

Lee Trevino

404

Skiing combines outdoor fun with knocking down trees with your face.

Dave Barry

405

If you are going to try cross-country skiing, start with a small country.

From "Saturday Night Live"

406

Yell for a Virginia high school:

We don't drink!
We don't smoke!
Norfolk!

Unknown

407

Fishing is a delusion entirely surrounded by liars in old clothes.

Don Marquis (1878–1937)

408

I bet on a horse at ten to one. It didn't come in until half-past five.

Henny Youngman

409

A good sport has to lose to prove it.

Unknown

410

As for bowling, how good can a thing be if it has to be done in an alley?

John Grigsby's ex-wife

411

When I feel athletic, I go to a sports bar.

Paul Clisura

412

Curiosity killed the cat, but for a while I was a suspect.

Steven Wright

413

It took me an hour to bury the cat, because it wouldn't stop moving.

From "The Monty Python Show"

414

Being a newspaper columnist is like being married to a nymphomaniac. It's great for the first two weeks.

Lewis Grizzard

415

As a novelist, I tell stories, and people give me money. Then financial planners tell me stories, and I give them money.

Martin Cruz Smith

416

The cure for writer's cramp is writer's block.

Inigo DeLeon

417

A painter can hang his pictures, but a writer can only hang himself.

Edward Dahlberg (1900–1977)

4 1 8

The multitude of books is a great evil. There is no limit to this fever for writing.

Martin Luther (1483–1546)

4 1 9

As she fell face down into the black muck of the mud-wrestling pit, her sweaty 300-pound opponent muttering soft curses in Latin on top of her, Sister Marie thought, "There is no doubt about it; the Pope has betrayed me."

Richard Savastio
Entry in San Jose State's bad writing contest, 1983

4 2 0

Desiree, the first female ape to go up in space, winked at me slyly and pouted her thick, rubbery lips unmistakably—the first of many such advances during what would prove to be the longest, most memorable space voyage of my career.

Martha Simpson
Entry in San Jose State's bad writing contest, 1985

421

Jake liked his women the way he liked his kiwi fruit;
sweet yet tart, firm-fleshed yet yielding to the touch,
and covered with short brown fuzzy hair.

Gretchen Schmidt
Entry in San Jose State's bad writing contest, 1989

422

Nice guys can't write.

Literary agent Knox Burger

423

If the doctor told me I had only six minutes to live, I'd
type a little faster.

Isaac Asimov

424

Writing books is certainly a most unpleasant occupa-
tion. It is lonesome, unsanitary, and maddening. Many
authors go crazy.

H. L. Mencken (1880–1956)

425

A blank page is God's way of showing you how hard it
is to be God.

Unknown

426

Either a writer doesn't want to talk about his work, or he
talks about it more than you want.

Anatole Broyard

In Ireland, a writer is looked upon as a failed conver-
sationalist.

Unknown

4 2 8

To call Richard Brautigan's poetry doggerel is an insult
to the entire canine world.

Lazlo Coakley

4 2 9

I am here to live out loud.

Emile Zola (1840–1902)

430

I sound my barbaric yawp from the rooftops of the world.
Walt Whitman (1819–1892)

431

Nothing stinks like a pile of unpublished writing.
Sylvia Plath (1932–1963)

432

No passion in the world is equal to the passion to alter someone else's draft.

H. G. Wells (1866–1946)

433

Having your book turned into a movie is like seeing your oxen turned into bouillon cubes.

John LeCarré

434

Writing is a profession in which you have to keep proving your talent to people who have none.
Jules Renard (1864–1910)

435

The relationship of editor to author is knife to throat.
Unknown

436

If I had more time, I would write a shorter letter.

Blaise Pascal (1623–1662)

437

Reading this book is like waiting for the first shoe to drop.

Ralph Novak

438

A book must be an ice ax to break the frozen sea within us.

Franz Kafka (1883–1924)

439

The New York Times Book Review is alive with the sound of axes grinding.

Gore Vidal

440

JFK—The Man and the Airport

Somebody's suggested book title

441

Nine-tenths of all existing books are nonsense.

Benjamin Disraeli (1804–1881)

Books for general reading always smell bad; the odor of common people hangs about them.

Friedrich Nietzsche (1844–1900)

Nietzsche was stupid and abnormal.

Leo Tolstoy (1828–1910)

[Tolstoy's *War and Peace* and *Anna Karenina* are] loose, baggy monsters.

Henry James (1843–1916)

Henry James writes fiction as if it were a painful duty.

Oscar Wilde (1854–1900)

I hate books, for they only teach people to talk about what they don't understand.

Jean-Jacques Rousseau (1712–1778)

Books should be tried by a judge and jury as though they were crimes.

Samuel Butler (1835–1902)

Has the net effect of the invention of printing been good or bad? I haven't the slightest idea and neither has anyone else. As well ask whether it was a good or a bad plan to give over so much of the world's space to oceans.

H. L. Mencken (1880–1956)

Autobiography is a preemptive strike against biographers.

Barbara Grizzuti Harrison

447

I haven't read any of the autobiographies about me.

Liz Taylor

448

I always read the last page of a book first so that if I die before I finish I'll know how it turned out.

Nora Ephron

449

I'm thirty years old, but I read at the thirty-four-year-old level.

Dana Carvey

450

When you watch television, you never see people watching television. We love television because it brings us a world in which television does not exist.

Barbara Ehrenreich

451

Hear no evil, speak no evil, see no evil, and you'll never be a television anchorman.

Dan Rather

452

Imagine what it would be like if TV actually were good. It would be the end of everything we know.

Marvin Minsky

453
America is a mistake, a giant mistake.

Sigmund Freud (1856–1939)

454
Making duplicate copies and computer printouts of things no one wanted even one of in the first place is giving America a new sense of purpose.

Andy Rooney

455
Americans will put up with anything provided it doesn't block traffic.

Dan Rather

456
Tips for Americans traveling abroad:
—Carry the Koran
—Paint a red dot on your forehead
—Wear sandals
—Never ask how the Mets are doing.

Mark Russell

457
The shortest distance between two points is usually under repair.

Unknown

458

If all the cars in the United States were placed end to end, it would probably be Labor Day Weekend.

Doug Larson

459

Parking is such street sorrow.

Herb Caen

460

The guy who invented the first wheel was an idiot. The guy who invented the other three, *he* was a genius.

Sid Caesar

461

A hick town is one in which there is no place to go where you shouldn't be.

Alexander Woollcott (1887–1943)

462

All creative people should be required to leave California for three months every year.

Gloria Swanson (1899–1983)

463

In some parts of the world, people still pray in the streets. In this country they're called pedestrians.

Gloria Pitzer

464

Nebraska is proof that Hell is full, and the dead walk the earth.

Liz Winston

465

You can always tell a Texan, but not much.

Unknown

466

Texans are proof that the world was populated by aliens.

Cynthia Nelms

467

Canada is the vichyssoise of nations—it's cold, half French, and difficult to stir.

Stuart Keate

468

I moved to Florida because you don't have to shovel water.

James "The Amazing" Randi

469

In Buffalo, suicide is redundant.

From A Chorus Line

470

Why don't some people just shoot themselves in the head the day they are born?

Arkady Renko

471

In Green Bay, Wisconsin, ten bowling shirts are considered a great wardrobe.

Greg Koch

4 7 2

Not as bad as you might have imagined.

Motto suggested for New Jersey by Calvin Trillin

4 7 3

Preferable to Youngstown.

Motto suggested for Akron, Ohio, by Calvin Trillin

4 7 4

A person who speaks good English in New York sounds like a foreigner.

Jackie Mason

4 7 5

New York is an exciting town where something is happening all the time, most of it unsolved.

Johnny Carson

4 7 6

An interesting thing about New York City is that the subways run through the sewers.

Garrison Keillor

477

On a New York subway you get fined for spitting, but you can throw up for nothing.

Lewis Grizzard

478

New York City is filled with the same kind of people I left New Jersey to get away from.

Fran Lebowitz

479

On New Year's Eve, people in New Jersey stay up till midnight and watch their hopes drop.

Richard Lewis

480

If you want to be safe on the streets at night, carry a projector and slides of your last vacation.

Helen Mundis

481

The top TV shows in Russia are "Bowling for Food" and "Wheel of Torture."

Yakov Smirnoff

482

The Russians love Brooke Shields because her eyebrows remind them of Leonid Brezhnev.

Robin Williams

483

Art is about making something out of nothing and selling it.

Frank Zappa

484

I do not seek, I find.

Pablo Picasso (1881–1973)

485

A thing of beauty is a joy for a while.

Hal Lee Luyah

486

I am a critic—as essential to the theater as ants to a picnic.

Joseph Mankiewicz

487

Without music, life would be a mistake.

Friedrich Nietzsche (1844–1900)

488

I have played over the music of that scoundrel Brahms. What a giftless bastard!

Peter Ilyich Tchaikovsky (1840–1893)

489

If Beethoven had been killed in a plane crash at the age of twenty-two, it would have changed the history of music . . . and of aviation.

Tom Stoppard

490

Bach in an hour. Offenbach sooner.

Sign on music store door

I was involved in the Great Folk Music Scare back in the sixties, when it almost caught on.

Martin Mull

We aren't worried about posterity; we want it to sound good right now.

Duke Ellington (1899–1974)

SONG TITLES:

"I Can't Get Over a Man like You, So You'll Have to Answer the Phone."

Melody Anne

"You're the Only Thing That's Rising in the Sour Dough of Life."

Maxine Edwards

"If I Had to Do It All Over Again, I'd Do It All Over You."

Abe Burrows

"Don't Sit Under the Apple Tree with Anyone Else but Me."

Isaac Newton (1642–1727), perhaps?

"I Gave Her a Ring, and She Gave Me the Finger."

Unknown

"I Can't Fall Asleep Since You Sat on My Pillow Last Night."

David E. Ortman

494

If it weren't for the Japanese and Germans, we wouldn't have any good war movies.

Stanley Ralph Ross

495

Old soldiers never die, just young ones.

Graffito

496

War is the unfolding of miscalculations.

Barbara Tuchman (1912–1989)

497

The war situation has developed not necessarily to Japan's advantage.

Emperor Hirohito (1901–1989), after losing two cities to atom bombs

498

Violence never solved anything.

Genghis Khan (1162–1227), according to Bob Lee

499

A doctor could make a million dollars if he could figure out a way to bring a boy into the world without a trigger finger.

Arthur Miller

500

When a thing is funny, search it carefully for a hidden truth.

George Bernard Shaw (1856–1950)

501

It's hard to be funny when you have to be clean.

Mae West (1892–1980)

502

I never had a sense of humor. What started me in a theatrical direction was finding at a very early age that I had a talent. I could impersonate chickens. Buk buk buk bacagh.

Jonathan Miller

5 0 3

You don't stop laughing because you grow old; you grow old because you stop laughing.

Michael Pritchard

5 0 4

Old age comes at a bad time.

Sue Banducci

5 0 5

After a certain age, if you don't wake up aching in every joint, you are probably dead.

Tommy Mein

5 0 6

If you survive long enough, you're revered—rather like an old building.

Katharine Hepburn

5 0 7

You know you're getting old when you stoop to tie your shoes and wonder what else you can do while you're down there.

George Burns

508

Old age means realizing you will never own all the dogs you wanted to.

Joe Gores

509

Children are a great comfort in your old age—and they help you reach it faster, too.

Lionel Kauffman

510

My grandmother started walking five miles a day when she was sixty. She's ninety-seven now, and we don't know where the hell she is.

Ellen DeGeneris

511

When I was young, the Dead Sea was still alive.

George Burns

512

My health is good; it's my age that's bad.

Ray Acuff at eighty-three

513

An old man in love is like a flower in winter.

Portuguese proverb

514

My parents didn't want to move to Florida, but they turned sixty, and it was the law.

Jerry Seinfeld

515

Never ask old people how they are if you have anything
else to do that day.

Joe Restivo

516

Death is not the end; there remains the litigation.

Ambrose Bierce (1842–1914)

517

If you don't go to other people's funerals, they won't go
to yours.

Unknown

518

Death is nature's way of saying, "Your table is ready."

Robin Williams

519

Grave, n. A place in which the dead are laid to await the
coming of the medical student.

Ambrose Bierce (1842–1914)

520

The old neighborhood has changed. Hurley Brothers
Funeral Home is now called Death 'n' Things.

Elmore Leonard

521

No matter how rich you become, how famous or powerful, when you die the size of your funeral will still pretty much depend on the weather.

Michael Pritchard

522

Death sneaks up on you like a windshield sneaks up on a bug.

Unknown

523

The wages of sin are death, but by the time taxes are taken out, it's just sort of a tired feeling.

Paula Poundstone

524

Get out of here and leave me alone. Last words are for fools who haven't said enough already.

Last words of Karl Marx (1818–1883), allegedly

525

Errol Flynn died on a seventy-foot yacht with a seventeen-year-old girl. Walter's always wanted to go that way, but he's going to settle for a seventeen-footer and a seventy-year-old.

Mrs. Walter Cronkite

526

I don't want to achieve immortality by being inducted
into baseball's Hall of Fame. I want to achieve immortality by not dying.

Leo Durocher at eighty-one

527

LAST WILL AND TESTAMENT:
I owe much, I have nothing, the rest I leave to the poor.

Rabelais (1494–1553)

528

Exercise daily. Eat wisely. Die anyway.

Unknown

PART THREE

One thing and another

529

I really didn't say everything I said.

Yogi Berra

530

Next to the originator of a great quote is the first quoter of it.

Ralph Waldo Emerson (1803–1882)

531

A committee is a group of important individuals who singly can do nothing but who can together agree that nothing can be done.

Fred Allen (1894–1956)

532

Diplomacy is the art of letting someone else have your way.

Unknown

533

Palm Springs University—more than one hundred degrees available.

Unknown

534

The trouble with England is that it's all pomp and no circumstance.

From the 1954 movie Beat the Devil

535

You can be sincere and still be stupid.

Unknown

536

I felt sorry for myself because I had no hands until I met a man who had no chips.

Kent G. Andersson

537

Make a bet every day, otherwise you might walk around
lucky and never know it.

Jimmy Jones

538

I bear no grudges. I have a mind that retains nothing.

Bette Midler

539

Go to the zoo and enlist. Shave your neighbor's dog. Yo!
Dump your spaghetti on that guy's head.

*Inside the ears of crazy people with
cartoonist Gary Larson*

540
Two leaps per chasm is fatal.

Chinese proverb

541

People who sell macramé should be dyed a natural color and hung out to dry.

Calvin Trillin

542

The only thing standing between you and a watery grave is your wits, and that's not my idea of adequate protection.

From the movie Beat the Devil, *1954*

543

If the rich could hire people to die for them, the poor could make a wonderful living.

Jewish proverb

544

My karma ran over your dogma.

Unknown

545

Flying is hours and hours of boredom sprinkled with a few seconds of sheer terror.

Gregory "Pappy" Boyington

546

There is nothing worse than a "now" look with a "then" face.

Dave Falk

547

Prejudices save time.

Robert Byrne

548

The prime purpose of eloquence is to keep other people from talking.

Louis Vermeil

549

There are some things only intellectuals are crazy enough to believe.

George Orwell (1903–1950)

550

People performing mime in public should be subject to citizen's arrest on the theory that the normal First Amendment protection of free speech has in effect been waived by someone who has formally adopted a policy of not speaking.

Calvin Trillin

551

If you shoot at mimes, should you use a silencer?

Steven Wright

552

It is easier for a camel to pass through the eye of a needle if it is lightly greased.

John Nesvig

553

Time flies like an arrow.
Fruit flies like a banana.

Lisa Grossman

554

She had the Midas touch. Everything she touched turned into a muffler.

Lisa Smerling

555

I've always found paranoia to be a perfectly defensible position.

Pat Conroy

556

The early worm gets caught.

John Igo

557

Familiarity breeds contempt, but you can't breed without familiarity.

Maxim Kavolik

558

Familiarity breeds children.

Mark Twain (1835–1910)

559

Two heads are better than none.

Jean Green

560

The best car safety device is a rear-view mirror with a cop in it.

Dudley Moore

561

Leroy is a self-made man, which shows what happens when you don't follow directions.

Cartoon caption by Bill Hoest

5 6 2

If Noah had been truly wise
He would have swatted those two flies.

H. Castle

5 6 3

The fuchsia is the world's most carefully spelled flower.

Jimmy Barnes

5 6 4

I had a prejudice against the British until I discovered that fifty percent of them were female.

Raymond Floyd

5 6 5

Washington Irving.
Answer to the question "Who was the first president, Max?"

Steve Allen's Question Man

5 6 6

Any other last requests?
Answer to the question "Would you mind not smoking?"

Unknown

567

Wise men talk because they have something to say; fools talk because they have to say something.

Plato (427–347 B.C.)

Plato was a bore.

Friedrich Nietzsche (1844–1900)

568

Nietzsche is pietsche,
But Sartre is smartre.

Unknown

Nietzsche was stupid and abnormal.

Leo Tolstoy (1828–1910)

569

Help! I'm being held prisoner by my heredity and environment!

Dennis Allen

570

Drawing on my fine command of the English language, I said nothing.

Robert Benchley (1889–1945)

571

GREAT MOMENTS IN HISTORY:
    January 17, 1821: First recorded incident of a bird
        mistaking a civil servant for a statue.
    Second Recorded Incident

5 7 2

The days of the digital watch are numbered.

Tom Stoppard

5 7 3

I have never seen a situation so dismal that a policeman couldn't make it worse.

Brendan Behan (1923–1964)

5 7 4

A clear conscience is often the sign of a bad memory.

Unknown

5 7 5

Praise does wonders for the sense of hearing.

Unknown

5 7 6

If I die, I forgive you; if I live, we'll see.

Spanish proverb

5 7 7

A pedestrian is a man whose son is home from college.

Unknown

5 7 8

Most conversations are simply monologues delivered in the presence of witnesses.

Margaret Millar

579

She's descended from a long line her mother listened to.

Gypsy Rose Lee (1914–1970)

580

Confusion is always the most honest response.

Marty Indik

581

I'm not confused, I'm just well-mixed.

Robert Frost (1874–1963)

582

Does the name Pavlov ring a bell?

Unknown

583

If at first you don't succeed, you're about average.

Unknown

584

Who's Bob?
What to reply to a person who says, "I'm so confused, Bob."

John Grimes

585

I was walking down the street wearing glasses when the prescription ran out.

Steven Wright

586

When I can no longer bear to think of the victims of broken homes, I begin to think of the victims of intact ones.

Peter De Vries

587

Have you always been a Negro or are you just trying to be fashionable?

From the television series "Julia"

588

If I had permission to do everything, I wouldn't want to do anything.

The one best thing Joe Palen ever said

589

Thou shalt not admit adultery.

Hal Lee Luyah

590

There's a deception to every rule.

Hal Lee Luyah

591

Easy Street is a blind alley.

Unknown

592

To disagree with three-fourths of the British public is one of the first requisites of sanity.

Oscar Wilde (1854–1900)

593

There are two kinds of complainers, men and women.

Unknown

There are two kinds of people, those who finish what they start and so on.

Robert Byrne

595

A hat should be taken off when you greet a lady and left off for the rest of your life. Nothing looks more stupid than a hat.

P. J. O'Rourke

596

Toys are made in heaven, batteries are made in hell.

Tom Robbins

597

I bought some batteries, but they weren't included.

Steven Wright

598

There's never enough time to do all the nothing you want.

Bill Watterson

599

Quote me if I'm wrong.

Unknown

600

The only thing I can't stand is discomfort.

Gloria Steinem

601

Oh, well, half of one, six dozen of the other.

Joe Garagiola

602

The trouble with dawn is that it comes too early in the day.

Susan Richman

603

When I think over what I have said, I envy dumb people.

Seneca (4 B.C.–A.D. 65)

604

What kills a skunk is the publicity it gives itself.

Abraham Lincoln (1809–1865)

605

If you have any problems at all, don't hesitate to shut up.

Robert Mankoff

606

Fear is that little darkroom where negatives are developed.

Michael Pritchard

607

Last night somebody broke into my apartment and replaced everything with exact duplicates. When I pointed it out to my roommate, he said, "Do I know you?"

Steven Wright

608

The town where I grew up has a zip code of E-I-E-I-O.

Martin Mull

609

They should put expiration dates on clothes so we would
know when they go out of style.

Garry Shandling

610

Confidence is always overconfidence.

Robert Byrne

611

Lucy: Do you think anybody ever really changes?
Linus: I've changed a lot in the last year.
Lucy: I mean for the better.

Charles Schulz

612

The major concerns of Emily Litella:
1. Conservation of national race horses
2. Violins on television
3. Soviet jewelry
4. Endangered feces.

Gilda Radner (1946–1989)

613

Let a smile be your umbrella, because you're going to get soaked anyway.

Unknown

614

Gravity isn't easy, but it's the law.

Unknown

615

Queen Elizabeth is the whitest person in the world.

Bette Midler

616

Everybody is who he was in high school.

Calvin Trillin

617

I got kicked out of ballet class because I pulled a groin muscle, even though it wasn't mine.

Rita Rudner

618

Open your mouth only to change feet.

Stanley Ralph Ross

619

Gentiles are people who eat mayonnaise for no reason.

Robin Williams

620

Some guy hit my fender, and I said to him, "Be fruitful and multiply," but not in those words.

Woody Allen

621

The turn of the century will probably be made by a woman.

Unknown

622

Isn't Muamar Khadafy the sound a cow makes when sneezing?

Dave Barry

623

All Ireland is washed by the Gulf Stream, except my wife's family.

Brendan Behan (1923–1964)

624

Keep things as they are—vote for the Sado-Masochistic Party.

Unknown

625

He who lives far from neighbors may safely praise himself.

Erasmus (1466–1536)

626

Astrology is not an art, it is a disease.

Maimonides (1135–1204)

627

The closest anyone ever comes to perfection is on a job application form.

Unknown

628

Capital punishment is our society's recognition of the sanctity of human life.

Senator Orrin Hatch of Utah

629

So much work, so few women to do it.

Unknown

630

I'm not a Jew. I'm Jew*ish*. I don't go the whole hog.

Jonathan Miller

631

On Golden Blond.

Porn video title

632

I locked my keys in the car and had to break the windshield to get my wife out.

Red Skelton

633

Prostitution, like acting, is being ruined by amateurs.

Alexander Woollcott (1887–1943)

634

A good husband is healthy and absent.

Japanese proverb

635

WYMI—the all-philosophy radio station.

Mike Dugan

636

No man should plant more garden than his wife can hoe.

Old saying

637

If you have something of importance to say, for God's sake start at the end.

Sarah Jeannette Duncan

Sources, References, and Notes

Quotes are listed here only when there is something useful to add; the details given are all I have. Readers with fuller information are urged to write to me in care of Atheneum Publishers, 866 Third Avenue, New York, New York 10022.

1. EB as quoted by Charles Roos in *The Rocky Mountain News*, August 31, 1986.
2. MD as quoted in *Rave* magazine, November 1986.
3. AE as quoted by Herb Caen in *The San Francisco Chronicle*, May 16, 1989.
4. WHA as quoted by Dear Abby in her column, May 16, 1988.
8. MR in the Introduction to his *The Best of Modern Humor*, Knopf, 1983.
10. LT and JW in *The Search for Intelligent Life in the Universe*.
12. Russian proverb quoted by R. W. Payne in *A Stress Analysis of a Strapless Evening Gown*, 1963.
14. RR as quoted by Alec Guinness in his autobiography, 1986.
15. Unknown, thanks to Rothwell D. Mason.
16. Unknown, as quoted in *The Hayward Daily Review*, February 18, 1986.
25. LW in a letter to RB.
27. Unknown, thanks to Marqua Lee Brunette.
30. KN on "Saturday Night Live."
32. EP, thanks to R. G. Fisher.
33. EW as quoted in *The San Francisco Chronicle*, April 8, 1989.
35. Unknown, thanks to Eliza Sunneland.

36. FK as quoted by Leah Garchick in *The San Francisco Chronicle*, August 21, 1988.

39. Osage saying thanks to Bob Lee.

40. KN as quoted by Herb Caen in *The San Francisco Chronicle*, August 10, 1985.

41. RWW as quoted in *The Journal of Irreproducible Results*, 1985.

42. AS in *The San Francisco Examiner*.

49. SR, thanks to C. Wesley Eicole, M.D.

51. LT and JW in *The Search for Intelligent Life in the Universe*.

53. SG as quoted by A. Scott Berg in *Goldwyn*, 1989.

54. Irish saying, thanks to Richard Meehan.

58. Unknown, thanks to Stephan Adams.

61. MF as quoted in *The Journal of Irreproducible Results*, 1985.

68. FW in *Down Among the Women*.

70. MW in the movie *Belle of the Nineties*, 1934.

75. BY, thanks to Robert C. Smith.

76. GU, thanks to Johnson Letellier.

78. JM in *The Chicago Sun-Times*, November 9, 1986.

81. RS in *The San Francisco Chronicle*, August 15, 1988.

88. DB is a syndicated columnist for *The Miami Herald*.

89. From TU's television show, May 5, 1989.

90. AH is a standup comedian.

92. PD as quoted by Milton Berle in *B.S. I Love You*, McGraw-Hill, 1988.

94. TS is a standup comedian.

95. SL, thanks to Emily Smith.

96. RB as quoted by Jon Carroll in *The San Francisco Chronicle*, April 1, 1986.

102. KB in a letter from the front, 1943.

103. JS, thanks to John Diones.

106. AL, thanks to John Grigsby.

109. WA in *The Lunatic's Tale*, 1986.

110. JBB is a syndicated columnist.

111. RR is a standup comedian.

112. DP in *A Telephone Call*.

113. JR is a standup comedian.
115. JT is a standup comedian.
117. MP writes for *The Providence Journal*.
134. Thanks to Dr. Win Bottom.
140. WA in the movie *Manhattan*, 1979.
142. JH in *Good as Gold*, 1979.
145. NS in *Brighton Beach Memoirs*, 1986.
146. WA in the movie *A Midsummer Night's Sex Comedy*, 1982.
147. From the show that aired October 7, 1987.
148. LB is a standup comedian.
150. LG in *Elvis Is Dead and I Don't Feel So Good Myself*, 1987.
152. Censors cut this MW line from *Every Day's a Holiday*, 1937.
153. JK in *People Will Talk*, 1986.
154. WD is a standup comedian.
155. KW in *Billy Liar on the Moon*, 1975.
158. From MG's cartoon strip "Life Is Hell."
161. AC is a standup comedian.
166. GG in *Playboy*, June 1989.
167. WA in *The Lunatic's Tale*, 1986.
177. Screenplay by Laurie Craig.
178. DB in *Florida* magazine.
179. DC is a standup comedian.
184. Q is a French writer quoted by Peter De Vries in *Into Your Tent I'll Creep*, 1971.
187. LG as quoted by Liz Smith in her syndicated column, October 27, 1987.
188. Unknown, thanks to Robert G. Smith.
192. RLS, thanks to Susan Trott.
194. From the television show "All in the Family."
195. SV is a standup comedian.
198. ML as quoted by Jeanne Wearing on KPOF, Denver, October 1986.
199. MJF as quoted by Leah Garchick in *The San Francisco Chronicle*, January 27, 1988.
200. BC in *Love and Marriage*, 1989.

201. RD in *Rave*, November 1986.

205. WA in *The Lunatic's Tale*, 1986.

207. SJ as quoted by Herb Caen in *The San Francisco Chronicle*, February 3, 1986.

208. TG as quoted by Herb Caen in *The San Francisco Chronicle*, February 3, 1986.

212. HC in *The San Francisco Chronicle*, June 13, 1986.

227. GK in a lecture at College of Marin (Kentfield, California), January 12, 1989.

229. EP as quoted by Guy Trebay in *The Village Voice*, January 7, 1985.

234. CL is a standup comedian.

239. FO'C as quoted by Mark Childress in *The New York Times Book Review*, May 21, 1989.

242. BH on "The Tonight Show," January 2, 1987.

243. RR is a standup comedian.

247. Unknown, thanks to Henry Crossfield.

248. RS's grandfather as quoted in RS's *Yes, My Darling Daughter*, 1976.

250. PK as quoted by J. Bryan, III in *Hodgepodge Two*, Atheneum, 1989.

251. Unknown, as quoted by Herb Caen in *The San Francisco Chronicle*, December 22, 1987.

258. Tribesman quoted by Margaret Mead in *Male and Female*, 1949.

264. CL is a standup comedian.

265. MS is a standup comedian.

268. CC, thanks to Bill McCollough.

270. TE as quoted by D. Fischer in *Historians' Fallacies*, 1970.

271. JM in *The Rocky Mountain News*.

272. PP is a standup comedian.

273. Unknown, as quoted by Ray Orrock in *The Hayward Daily Review*, February 28, 1986.

276. BA as quoted by Herb Caen in *The San Francisco Chronicle*, May 6, 1986.

277. MD, thanks to John Grigsby.

281. BL is a sports columnist for the *Philadelphia Inquirer*.

283. BC as quoted by Rob Morse in *The San Francisco Examiner*, June 1, 1986.

289. Unknown, thanks to Lee Simon.

290. GS as quoted by Herb Caen, *The San Francisco Chronicle*, December 22, 1987.

292. From TA's 1975 movie *Lies My Father Told Me*.

299. RSW in *The San Francisco Chronicle*, June 5, 1986.

305. DD, thanks to Marty Indik.

306. DM as quoted in *The New York Times Book Review*, December 29, 1985.

308. CM in *The San Francisco Examiner*, July 20, 1986.

310. JM in *The San Francisco Chronicle*, November 30, 1988.

313. NWJ in a letter to RB.

317. GN in *The San Francisco Chronicle*, May 18, 1989.

318. OW in *People*, March 6, 1989.

319. RQ, Cyra McFadden's former stepfather, as quoted in her *Rain or Shine*, 1986.

320. AW, thanks to Robert G. Smith.

322. JH is a standup comedian.

323. JH, thanks to Marty Indik.

325. Tribesman quoted by Jared Diamond in *Discover*, May 1987.

328. AC is a standup comedian.

330. AWB is a standup comedian.

333. JL as quoted by Herb Caen in *The San Francisco Chronicle*, March 3, 1986.

334. SJ as quoted by Herb Caen in *The San Francisco Chronicle*, July 10, 1988.

342. MP as quoted in *Miss Piggy's Guide to Life*, as told to Henry Beard, 1981.

343. EL to RB.

344. MO'D as quoted by Paul Slansky in *Playboy*, 1989.

345. MB as quoted in *Playboy*, 1975.

346. JB as quoted by Edward S. Gifford, Jr., in *He's My Boy*, 1962.

347. Unknown, thanks to Jim Eason.

358. JKG in *Ambassador's Journal*, 1969.

359. RP in *L'Habit Vert*, 1912.

368. EP as quoted by Guy Trebay in *The Village Voice*, January 7, 1985.

369. On Cable News Network, April 26, 1988.

370. GV, thanks to Stefan D. Koch, who was his student at Temple University.

372. As quoted by Carlos Fuentes in *The New York Times Book Review*, April 6, 1986.

373. As quoted by Dale McFeathers of the Scripps Howard News Service.

376. Cartoon caption by JM in *The New Yorker*, April 3, 1989.

379. BM is a television newsman in Oakland, California.

382. JL as quoted in *Esquire*, December 1986.

383. HK as quoted in *The Miami Herald*, January 3, 1987.

386. JL as quoted in *Esquire*, December 1986.

387. GV, thanks to Bill Weiss.

388. PW-D to RB.

389. SG as quoted in *The Moguls* by Norman Zierold, 1969.

392. DB, thanks to Johnson Letellier.

393. MM as quoted by Herb Caen in *The San Francisco Chronicle*, January 1, 1985.

395. GE as quoted by Jake Curtis in *The San Francisco Chronicle*, August 31, 1987.

396. TB in his cartoon strip "Funky Winkerbean."

397. DJ as quoted in *Boring Stuff* by Alan Caruba.

398. SO in *The Los Angeles Times*, November 1988.

399. From a column by Art Rosenbaum in *The San Francisco Chronicle*, January 20, 1988.

403. LT on "The Tonight Show," January 1985.

406. I remember this pep yell from the 1950s.

408. HY as quoted by Milton Berle in *B.S. I Love You*, 1988.

409. Unknown, thanks to Jason Olive.

411. PC as quoted by Herb Caen in *The San Francisco Chronicle*, July 11, 1988.

414. LG, thanks to Susan Richman.

415. MCS to RB.

416. ID as quoted by Herb Caen in *The San Francisco Chronicle*, August 15, 1988.

418. ML in *Table Talk*.

424. HLM at the 1940 convention of the American Booksellers Association.

425. Unknown, as quoted by Milton Berle in *B.S. I Love You*, 1988.

426. AB in *The New York Times Book Review*, May 21, 1989.

428. LC in a letter to *The San Francisco Chronicle*, February 9, 1988.

432. HGW as quoted by Macdonald Carey in *The Writers Guild of America News*, May 1986.

433. JL, thanks to Karl Fulves.

435. Unknown, thanks to Karl Fulves.

437. RN in *People* reviewing a book by Judith Michael.

438. FK in a letter written when he was twenty.

439. GV as quoted by David Show in *The Los Angeles Times*, December 12, 1985.

441. BD in *Lothair*, 1870.

442. FN in *Beyond Good and Evil*.

443. JJR in *Emile*.

444. SB in *Note Books*.

445. HLM at the 1940 convention of the American Booksellers Association.

446. BGH on the television program "Bookmark," April 2, 1989.

447. LT on "The Donahue Show," February 12, 1988.

448. A line from the movie *When Harry Met Sally*, 1989, screenplay by NE.

450. BE in *Mother Jones*.

451. DR as quoted in *The National Enquirer*, January 17, 1987.

452. MM as quoted in *The New York Times Book Review*, September 27, 1987.

455. DR, thanks to Bob Cudmore.

457. Unknown, as quoted by Ray Orrock in *The Hayward Daily Review*.

460. SC as quoted by Milton Berle in *B.S. I Love You*, 1988.

463. GP, thanks to John Grigsby.

465. Unknown, thanks to Jim Eason.

468. JR as quoted in *Money* magazine, September 1986.

470. AR is a character in *Gorky Park* (1981) and *Polar Star* (1989), novels by Martin Cruz Smith published by Random House.

471. GK made the remark after being traded by the Green Bay Packers to the Miami Dolphins.

475. JC on his 25th Anniversary Show, September 25, 1986.

476. From a lecture by GK at College of Marin (Kentfield, California), January 12, 1989.

478. FL as quoted in *Rave*, November 1986.

481. YS as quoted in *Rave*, November 1986.

483. FZ in *Money* magazine, September 1986.

486. From JM's 1950 screenplay for *All About Eve*, a movie based on a short story by Mary Orr.

490. As quoted by Joseph Gallagher in *The Baltimore Sun*, October 12, 1988.

495. Graffito, thanks to Stefan D. Koch.

497. H as quoted by John Toland in *The Rising Sun;* thanks to Robert Gordon.

498. GK, thanks to Bob Lee.

502. JM quoted in *The New Yorker*, April 17, 1989.

503. MP, thanks to Jim Eason.

504. SB as quoted by Herb Caen in *The San Francisco Chronicle*, April 9, 1989.

505. TM as quoted by Herb Caen in *The San Francisco Chronicle*, January 6, 1986.

510. ED is a standup comedian.

520. EL in *Glitz*.

522. Unknown, thanks to Stefan D. Koch.

524. KM, thanks to Jason Olive.

526. LD as quoted in *The San Francisco Chronicle*, July 27, 1989.

529. YB as quoted by George Will in *Newsweek*, April 14, 1986.

531. FA as quoted by J. Bryan, III in *Merry Gentlemen (and One Lady)*, 1985.

532. Unknown, thanks to Susan Richman.

534. Screenplay by Truman Capote and John Huston.

537. JJ is a horse trainer quoted by William Murray in *When the Fat Man Sings*, 1987.

540. Chinese proverb thanks to Michele Plunkett.

542. Screenplay by Truman Capote and John Huston.

545. GB shot down twenty-four Japanese planes in WWII.

546. DF as quoted by Herb Caen in *The San Francisco Chronicle*, December 6, 1987.

548. LV as quoted in *Forbes*, April 17, 1987.

549. GO as quoted by Alexander Bloom in *Prodigal Sons*, Oxford University Press, 1986.

550. CT in *The New Yorker*, May 15, 1989.

552. JN, thanks to Johnson Letellier.

554. LS, thanks to Kris Chotzinoff.

555. PC, from his novel *Prince of Tides*, 1986.

557. MK as quoted in *Perfect Pitch* by Nicolas Slonimsky, 1988.

559. JG, thanks to Susan Richman.

562. HC, thanks to John Grigsby.

563. JB as quoted by Herb Caen in *The San Francisco Chronicle*, August 9, 1988.

567. P, thanks to Bill McCollough.

569. DA in a letter to RB.

581. RF as quoted by Charles Roos in *The Rocky Mountain News*, September 26, 1986.

582. Unknown, thanks to Jason Olive.

587. Screenwriter: Alvin Sargent. Thanks to Jack Mingo.

591. Unknown, thanks to Jason Olive.

595. PJO'R in *Modern Manners*, 1988.

596. TR as quoted in *The San Francisco Examiner*, September 28, 1987. Thanks to Michael O. Stearns.

600. GS, thanks to Blair Chotzinoff.

611. From a "Peanuts" comic strip, March 28, 1989.

612. GR on "Saturday Night Live."

617. RR is a standup comedian.
621. The quote is sometimes credited to the late film star Alan Ladd.
622. DB as quoted by Herb Caen in *The San Francisco Chronicle*, April 22, 1986.
625. E in *In Praise of Folly*.

Index of Authors

Index of Subjects and Key Words

ABOUT THE AUTHOR

After the publication of his previous book of quotations, **Robert Byrne** was jailed for petty theft (he argued for grand theft) and is serving a sentence of 637 days at a Hallmark card store in Vermin, Utah. "Till now," he postcards lamely, "sentences had always served *me*." The author of sixteen books, he is presently working on alibis.